Jackrabbit

Snowy owl

Harvest mice

ANIMAL BITES

animals on the move

Dorothea DePrisco

Striped dolphins

how to use this book

Look for these colorful tabs to guide your Animal Bites adventure.

how they move Discover different ways animals move

african elephant When you see a tab this color, get a close-up look at amazing animals

why they move Learn the reasons animals move from place to place

vista See awesome photos that show the places animals live

big data Find the facts and figures

animal gallery Take a look at animal similarities and differences

where they live Explore different animal habitats and ecosystems

working Find out different ways people interact with animals and their habitats

Just like me
Look for this feature to see how animals behave and live like humans.

table of contents

Homes and hangouts

In the air

Animals hang out in places that have what they need to survive. Birds, insects, and just one kind of mammal—bats—fly through the sky.

Flying fox

Bumblebee

Dragonfly

Giraffe

On the ground

Mammals, many reptiles and amphibians, and some insects and arachnids (like spiders) live on the ground and in plants and trees.

White corded standard poodle

Scottish fold

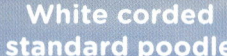

Underground

Many amphibians, some reptiles and insects, and some mammals live in burrows and underground homes.

Shovel-nosed snake

Red ant

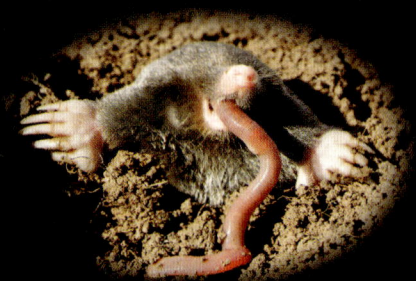
Mole and worm

Nine-banded armadillo

Great blue heron

Swallowtail butterfly

Coypu

Red claw scorpion

Fire salamander

Mole cricket

In the water

Fish, marine mammals (like whales and dolphins), and some invertebrates (animals without a backbone, like octopuses) swim in watery places.

Leopard shark

Unicorn fish

Piranha

Leopard torpedo ray

Reef octopus

Red sea urchin

European otter

Ready to go

Animals move in their own special ways. Some hang, some glide, and others swim or climb. They all have parts that help them get around. Some have amazing extra talents, as well.

Toe-rrific

The common chameleon has large toes that help it grip branches and a prehensile tail it uses for balance.

Ocean motion

Sea stars have feet . . . on their arms! They push the feet out and pull them back in to move. The feet also act like suction cups to help them stay put in strong ocean currents.

Eye see you

The crested serpent eagle's large eyes help them spot prey, including snakes, other reptiles, and rodents, while soaring high above the ground.

Paws and claws

Cats can flex a muscle to push their claws out. Since cats walk on their toes, they usually keep their claws in for comfort.

The tale of a tail

The red howler monkey's tail is longer than its whole body. It is prehensile, which means it can be used like an extra hand to grab and hold onto things.

Catch me if you can

Cheetahs are the fastest land animals. They can run up to 70 miles per hour. But they can only maintain this speed for short bursts—if they don't catch their food right away, they will give up on a chase.

The **tail** is used for balance and steering while making fast turns.

Huge **leg muscles** provide extra power.

INFO BITES

Name: Cheetah

Type of animal: Mammal

Home: Eastern, Central, Southwestern Africa, plus Iran

Size: Up to 3 feet tall (at the shoulder) and 46 to 159 pounds.

Moving fact: Cheetahs run so fast, they have to slow down when they catch up to their prey. They can slow down even faster than they can accelerate.

The **spine** is flexible, allowing it to turn its body in midair.

The **heart, lungs,** and **nostrils** work together to take in the oxygen needed to run fast.

Sunlight bounces off **black tear marks**, making it easier to see prey.

Just like me

Cheetah moms take good care of their babies. They keep their cubs safe and make sure they have enough food to eat.

GOOD TEAMMATE?

☐ YES   ☒ NO

Cheetahs are fast and would win any race they enter, but they're solitary creatures—they like to be alone.

On your mark . . . get set . . . go!

Animals in the wild run to catch food, escape danger, and move quickly from place to place. They have all the right body parts, strength, and flexibility to get around at high speeds.

Small and fast

Red foxes are small—about the size of a small dog. They have slim bodies, which help them run fast. They can reach speeds of up to 45 miles per hour.

Quick turns

The European red squirrel can rotate its ankles and feet in any direction. This means they can turn around while the squirrel is running. So if it sees something it doesn't like, it can quickly change direction.

On the surface

The basilisk lizard can run on water. Why doesn't it sink? Its large back feet have flaps of skin between each toe. It spreads out its toes to trap air, which keeps it on the surface.

Giddyup!

Horses run at different speeds by moving their legs in a variety of patterns, called gaits. These include walking, trotting, cantering, and galloping. Horses can start off on either their right or left leg.

There and back again

Animals of all kinds migrate, which means they travel long distances each year. They move to find food, to leave behind cold weather, or to find a safe place to give birth. Migrating animals get where they need to go alone or in groups.

Cooperation

American white pelicans spend their summers on inland lakes. They head south in the winter, where they gather in large colonies by the seashore.

ROAD CLOSED
RED CRAB MIGRATION
NO ENTRY BY VEHICLES
BEYOND THIS POINT

Getting crabby

Every year, millions of red crabs on Christmas Island in Australia travel to the sea to mate. They walk through towns, houses, and over roads. When they reach the ocean, they take a quick dip. Then they dig burrows in the sand, where the females will lay eggs.

Familiar route

Free-ranging American bison herds follow the same path when they migrate every year. In winter snow, herds in Yellowstone National Park travel from their summer ranges to winter ranges in search of food.

Winging it

Some dragonflies travel south for the winter, looking for warmer weather. The globe skimmer makes an 11,000-mile journey from India to Africa—the longest migration in the insect world. For dragonflies, it's a one-way trip.

Baby nursery

Gray whales travel 10,000 miles, round-trip, every year. They leave the icy waters of the Arctic to give birth to their calves in the warm, shallow waters of Mexico. This is the longest migration of any mammal.

15

What's gnu with you?

The wildebeest is also called a gnu (pronounced "new"). It gallops like a horse, and acts like a bull, but is in fact an antelope. It waves its tail, bucks its head, and snorts. When it senses danger, it moves in a zigzag pattern to confuse a predator and escape.

Stripes make the **coat** look wrinkly from far away.

INFO BITES

Name: Blue Wildebeest

Type of animal: Mammal

Home: Eastern and Southern Africa

Size: Up to 57 inches tall (at the shoulder) and 500 to 600 pounds.

Moving fact: Wildebeests can kick up a dust storm when they spar. They push at one another with their horns. They call out "ge-nu," which is how they got their name.

Just like me
Just like human mothers, wildebeests take good care of their young, fighting off predators and outsiders.

The **tail** swishes back and forth to shoo away flies.

Hooves deliver heavy kicks to ward off predators.

Curved **horns** on both males and females are used in fights and self-defense.

GOOD NEIGHBOR?

☐ YES   ☒ NO

These animals migrate from the Masai Mara in Kenya to the Serengeti in Tanzania and back again. They are constantly moving and never stay anywhere for long.

Mommy day care

African elephant females and their young live together in large groups called herds. A herd is led by the oldest, and usually the largest, female. The older females in the group teach the young calves social and survival skills. Adult males, called bulls, live alone or in small groups.

Marco! Polo!

Whether swimming, drifting, or spinning, these aquatic animals know to how to keep moving. Animals that move through the water are built to make their way through fast currents, big waves, or quiet ponds.

That's deep

Marine animals can dive down deep into the ocean. The sperm whale can dive up to 6,500 feet below the surface to find something good to eat. It swims by moving its tail up and down.

Jet propulsion

Jellyfish often float along on ocean currents. To move quickly they squeeze their bell-shaped bodies to push water behind them and "jet" forward. It doesn't take a lot of energy to move this way.

In the swim

When you swim, do you do a frog kick? Add swim fins for webbed feet, and you can swim like a frog!

Swim class

Frogs that live in water use a powerful kick to move forward. Their legs are strong, but it's the webbed feet that do most of the work. Frogs that live on land don't have webbed feet.

Go for a spin

Spinner dolphins dive deep into the water, race to the surface, and spin in the air. Scientists think they may do this because they are happy, to get an animal such as a remora (a sucker fish) off their bodies, or to communicate with other dolphins.

Fin-tastic!

This fish has a sword for a nose, a torpedo-shaped body, and an amazing dorsal fin on top. The sailfish folds down this fin when it swims fast. It raises the fin to make itself look bigger when threatened.

The **tail** works to steer and turn.

INFo BITES

Name: Sailfish

Type of animal: Fish

Home: Atlantic and Indo-Pacific

Size: Up to 11 feet long and 220 pounds.

Moving fact: These fish often hunt together. They use their sails to bring schools of fish together for easy feasting.

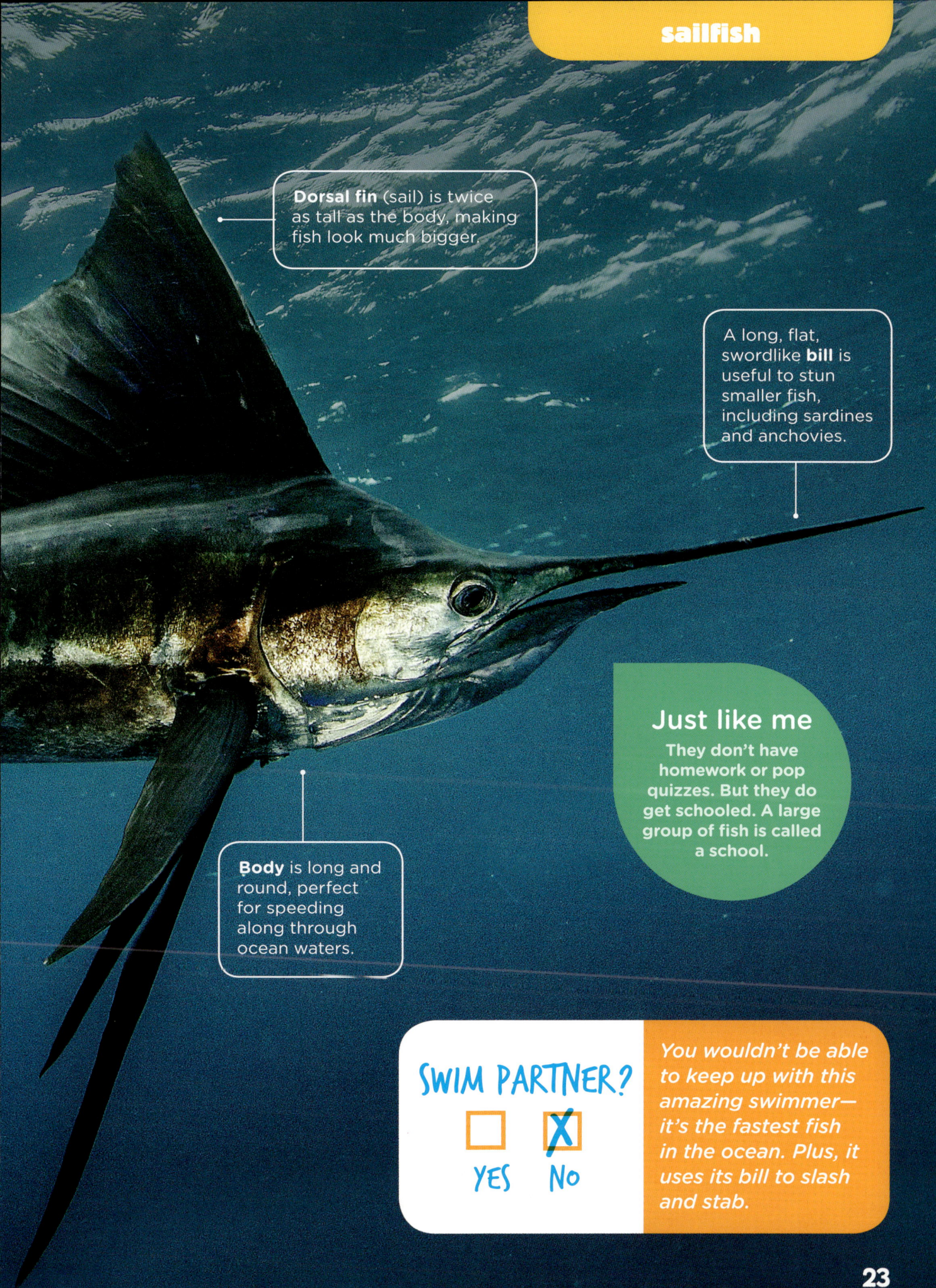

Dorsal fin (sail) is twice as tall as the body, making fish look much bigger.

A long, flat, swordlike **bill** is useful to stun smaller fish, including sardines and anchovies.

Just like me

They don't have homework or pop quizzes. But they do get schooled. A large group of fish is called a school.

Body is long and round, perfect for speeding along through ocean waters.

SWIM PARTNER?

☐ YES   ☒ No

You wouldn't be able to keep up with this amazing swimmer—it's the fastest fish in the ocean. Plus, it uses its bill to slash and stab.

Jack be nimble, Jack be quick!

These animals are known for their incredible jumping ability. From the smallest penguin in the Antarctic to the teeny, tiny flea, they all have ways of hopping and jumping without missing a single step.

Acrobatics

Himalayan blue sheep jump from cliff to cliff. Their hooves are soft and rubbery. This helps them maintain their balance in their high mountain home.

Tiny hopper

The kangaroo rat has small front legs designed for digging. The large toes on its long back legs help this 5-inch-long animal jump up to 9 feet in a single leap.

Slippery when wet

Adélie penguins can leap from water to land without slipping or sliding on the ice. They use their strong toenails to grip the ice and land safely.

Jump!

Fleas are incredible jumpers and can leap more than 100 times their own height. They have long back legs with springlike pads. These work like levers to push them through the air.

25

Taking it fast or slow

Speed demons

Slim bodies and large tails help ocean dwellers zoom through the ocean. Long legs and lean bodies help land dwellers run faster.

Mako shark

North African ostrich

American red squirrel

Loris

Millipede

Leopard sea cucumber

Golden silk orb weaver

Komodo dragon

Pronghorn

Aldabra giant tortoise

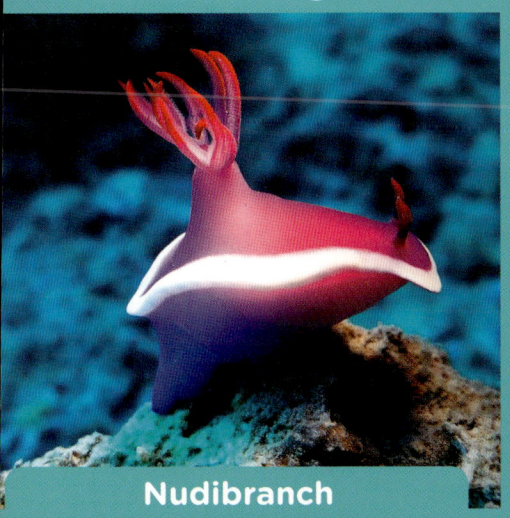

Nudibranch

Three-toed sloth

Slow movers

Slow pokes all have different ways of moving, but they have one thing in common. Try as they might, these creepers just aren't built for hurrying.

27

Leap into action

Like all insects, grasshoppers have three pairs of legs. Grasshoppers use their back legs, which are twice as long as the others, to jump. Meadow grasshoppers can jump 10 inches in the air. They can travel more than 3 feet in a single bound.

INFO BITES

Name: Meadow Grasshopper

Type of animal: Insect

Home: Canada, Northern United States, Europe, and Asia

Size: Up to 1 inch long.

Moving fact: A grasshopper can rub a leg against its body, rub a leg against a wing, or rub two wings to make different sounds.

Long **back legs** are used for jumping.

Antennae can smell and feel things.

Has two large **compound eyes** with three small **simple eyes** in between them.

Forewings are used for balance.

Four short **front legs** hold food, climb, and walk.

Just like me

Grasshoppers hear through the tympanum, a flat organ on their bellies near their back legs. Human eardrums are also called tympanum.

SINGING PAL?

YES   NO

Meadow grasshoppers use a series of clicks and buzzes when they sing. Each song lasts about five seconds, so you might need a lot of them to form a chorus.

On the hunt

Animals live where their food is. They move in different ways to get the food they need to survive.

Yellow recyclers

Banana slugs move slowly along the forest floor where they live, finding dead plants and fungi to eat. Sometimes, they don't move at all. During hot, dry weather, they cover themselves with mucus and burrow under moist leaves to protect themselves.

Hungry hunter

When fishers hunt, they travel alone. They are strong tree climbers, using their long claws to move quickly. They can also stretch out their bodies into burrows or hollow tree logs when looking for food. They are one of the few animals that can tackle a prickly porcupine.

Early risers

Jaguars are most active at dawn and dusk. They may stalk prey on the ground, or climb a tree and pounce on it from above. They also like water and swim after fish and caimans.

Floor walkers

Giant frogfish blend in with their coral reef surroundings. They wait there for small fish to swim by. Then, using the fins on the bottom of their body, they walk along the ocean floor to surprise— and eat—their prey.

Go fish

The cormorant is an expert fisher. This large bird chases fish underwater, using its webbed feet to swim through lakes, rivers, and oceans. Its long, thin, hooked bill is a perfect tool to catch and hold onto a tasty fish.

Mako my day

Its slim, tube-shaped body and powerful tail help this speedy shark swim up to 45 miles per hour. Swimming at high speeds, it can make spectacular leaps up to 20 feet out of the water.

Just like me
This shark relies on its senses to learn about its world, just like you do. It has good eyesight and an excellent sense of smell.

The crescent-shaped **tail** moves from side to side, propelling the shark forward.

INFO BITES

Name: Shortfin Mako

Type of animal: Fish

Home: Warm waters, worldwide

Size: Up to 13 feet long and 300 pounds.

Moving fact: The shortfin mako can travel thousands of miles in a single journey. An electronic tag on a shark's dorsal fin helps experts learn about its movement and travels.

Razor-sharp **teeth** grab prey and tear it into bite-sized chunks.

The **underbelly** is white, which makes it hard to spot from below.

SELFIE WORTHY?

[X] YES [X] NO

If you see this shark jumping out of the water, snap a pic quick. But don't get too close—those teeth are sharp!

Home is where the nest is

Some animals build homes where they live and raise their families, moving around only to look for food or a mate. Others build or borrow nests to give birth and raise their young. Some are quite large, others are small and cozy. They can be found in tree holes, hanging from branches, on telephone poles, and even underground.

High-rises

Termites are small, but they are mighty builders. They work together to create tall homes, called mounds, made of soil, termite saliva, and dung. At the bottom is a series of bubble-like chambers connected by passages, like rooms and hallways in a house.

What's the buzz?

Bees and wasps can build nests as big as a basketball. Each is made up of little chambers, or rooms, where larvae grow until they are ready to emerge as adults.

Damp dwellings

Bank voles give birth to their young in nests lined with grass and other plant matter. The nests are often found just below the surface, in the soft mud around tree roots.

Eager beavers

Beavers are master builders. They use their strong teeth to chew through tree trunks. They use the fallen branches to build homes, called lodges, and dams that can block streams. Beaver dams can be 10 feet high and up to 1,600 feet long.

Crafty cradle

Birds build nests using many different materials found in their habitats, including mud, twigs, leaves, and feathers. Nests built on tree branches offer protection from predators. Plus, it's easy for a parent to fly in with a yummy treat for dinner.

Nest mates

On a farm, barns offer safe nesting places for mice. A pile of hay makes a cozy crib. Baby mice—called pups or pinkies because of their color—are born without hair, so they cuddle up for warmth.

Up, up, and away!

How can some animals fly? Different animals have different ways of getting into the air. They each have body shapes and parts that help them soar. Not all flying animals have feathers.

Lifting off

Trumpeter swans are big, heavy birds. When they are ready to fly, they flap their feet and wings against the water. They flap and run for about 300 feet before they can lift off.

Fly away home

Ladybugs have a tough shell, called the elytra, covering each wing. It protects the wings until they are needed. When the ladybug flies, the elytra lift up and the wings unfold.

Would you like to go ballooning?

A ride in a hot air balloon lets you feel what it's like to float high above the ground.

Hang gliding

Flying lemurs have extra skin that stretches from their necks to their toes and tails, like a cape. When they spread out this skin flap, it helps them glide from tree to tree.

Swingers

When baby spiders want to travel, they go ballooning. They tip the middle of their bodies (the abdomen) toward the sky and release a silky web. The wind carries them through the air like a balloon.

The stackup

osprey

Up to 23 inches long and 4 pounds, wingspan up to 70 inches

TALENT: HOVERING

A hunting osprey flies slowly over water. When it spots a fish, it hovers, then dives down. It plunges feet first into the water to grab a fish in its talons.

great horned owl

Up to 25 inches long and 6 pounds, wingspan up to 57 inches

egyptian vulture

Up to 26 inches long and 5 pounds, wingspan up to 56 inches

TALENT: CLEVERNESS

This is one of the few animals that uses tools. When it spots an ostrich egg (or other large egg), it walks around to find a stone. It then throws the stone to crack the egg open and eat it.

golden eagle

Up to 33 inches long and 13 pounds, wingspan up to 96 inches

andean condor

Up to 49 inches long and 33 pounds, wingspan up to 120 inches

TALENT: FLYING HIGH

These heavy birds need help staying aloft. They glide on warm air currents, called thermals, in the mountainous areas where they live. They can soar for long periods of time, flapping their wings just once an hour.

TALENT: KEEPING QUIET

The great horned owl, like most owls, can flap its wings without making any sound. This, along with excellent vision and hearing, make it a stealthy hunter.

TALENT: HEAVY LIFTING

This bird can capture large prey. In fact, it's able to carry up to 8 pounds in its talons while flying. Some will even fight over food with bears and coyotes.

Stoop-endous!

This deep diver is the fastest animal in the world. Traveling at more than 200 miles per hour, it zooms straight down in a dive called a stoop. It can spot its dinner from as high as 3,500 feet and grab it in midair.

INFO BITES

Name: Peregrine Falcon

Type of animal: Bird

Home: Every continent except Antarctica

Size: Wingspan is 3 to 4 feet, and weight is 1 to 3 pounds.

Moving fact: Falcons shake their bodies. They do it to get dirt and dust off their feathers and smooth them out for flight.

Excellent **eyesight** helps locate prey from high above Earth.

The **hooked bill** is used to bite prey.

The **talons** and **claws** are used to attack and grab prey.

Just like me

Peregrine falcons communicate, making sounds called vocalizations. A couple will talk to each other and to their offspring, too.

PET WORTHY?

☐ YES ☒ No

Their name means "wanderer"—they need to fly free. And you'd need very high ceilings for those steep dives!

Good timing

How and where animals move helps them survive. Some travel to join larger groups for protection. Others find places where they can blend in. And some only move around at certain times when it is safe.

Home range

Coyotes generally live in family groups. Single males may form a bachelor group. Sometimes coyotes work together in a group to hunt a large animal. They establish a territory (an area for just their family) and defend it during denning season, when they raise their pups.

Branching out

Walking stick insects can be as short as an inch or longer than a foot. But all live on bushes or in trees. They look just like a branch or twig, making them masters of disguise.

Huddle up

Rats form a huddle to keep warm. The rats on the outer edge move to the middle, where it is cozy. Then they move back to the outside edge to give other family members time in the middle.

Sand art

When the tide goes out, sand bubbler crabs move quickly. They sift small bits of food from sand, leaving behind a dozen balls a minute. When the tide comes in, they dig burrows beneath the sand.

Sweet tooth

Honey badgers move frequently from place to place. They travel long distances to find food. They look for dens or other safe places to hide out, too.

Air and ocean motion

Flyers

The shape of an animal's wings determines how it flies. Pointed wings help an albatross glide through the air. A ladybug unfolds and flaps its wings to fly.

Common birdwing

Cape turtle dove

Waved albatross

Black edge moray eel

Bottlenose dolphin

Sulphur damsel

Three-spotted ladybug

Fruit bat

Bumblebee

Orca whale

Spotted eagle ray

Chum salmon

Swimmers

Fins and tails move swimmers through the water. Fish move their tails side to side, and mammals move them up and down. Side fins on whales help them steer left or right.

Take off!

Animals move in large groups for different reasons. Sometimes they move toward something—looking for food, mates, or new homes. Other times they're running away from something, such as a scary noise or nearby predators.

Stampeding

Horses, cattle, and other herd animals run together when something frightens them. It can be a loud clap of thunder or the smell of a nearby predator. This is called a stampede.

SWARMING

When large groups of insects travel together, it's called a swarm.

Honeybees

If a honeybee colony gets too big for its hive, it splits into two groups. One group flies off together to find a new home. They are less likely to sting when they are in a swarm, since they have no home to protect.

Army ants

Huge swarms of 100,000 or more army ants move across the rain forest, eating as they go. The ants use their enormous jaws to pierce skin, and they use teamwork to overpower animals much larger than themselves. Their prey includes insects, worms, and spiders.

Home on the range

Bison migrate in winter, looking for warmer weather and more plentiful food. Along the way, they use their heads like shovels and plow through deep snow to find tasty grasses to eat.

Doin' the twist

A sidewinder moves by lifting and twisting its body in an S-shape. Then it throws its looping midsection forward. This helps it move safely over hot desert sand.

GOOD BAND MEMBER?

☐ YES ☒ NO

A sidewinder can rattle like a rhythm section, but only when it's getting ready to bite.

The **buttons on the tail** make a rattling sound when shaken.

Scales on top of the body are raised and bumpy.

Just like me
Do you like to climb sand dunes? A sidewinder can climb, too. It lifts its head, then its tail, one after the other as it climbs.

Hornlike scales over the eyes act like a visor to block the sun and sand.

Heat pits help to sense nearby animals.

INFO BITES

Name: Sidewinder Snake

Type of animal: Reptile

Home: California, Arizona, Nevada, and Utah deserts, plus Mexico

Size: Up to 30 inches long and 7 ounces.

Moving fact: The sidewinder hunts by not moving at all. It buries itself in the desert sand and waits for a tasty lizard to pass by.

Do the locomotion

How do animals that don't have legs get around? They have special body parts that help them out, and clever ways of moving.

Slimed

The flat underbelly of a slug is called a foot, but it can't walk. It uses muscles to move its foot forward in a wavy motion. It releases a slimy jelly called mucus that protects the foot as it inches along.

Tusk, tusk!

How does a walrus move its enormous body on land? It uses its fins like feet to move forward, flopping its body up and down. It uses its tusks to pull itself out of the water onto land or ice.

Spine-tingling

Sea urchins use their long spines, tube feet, and teeth to walk on rocks and coral. They also use their teeth to chew through rocks to make a hiding place.

Stretch it out

The earthworm moves by stretching its body. It squeezes muscles to stretch out, then squeezes other muscles to scrunch up. It stretches and scrunches over and over to crawl forward.

Slow-comotion

Pythons have scales on their bellies that poke out like little knives. They use these to cling to the ground and pull themselves along.

Hop to it

Grey kangaroos can hop high and far. They move as fast as a car—up to 40 miles per hour. They travel in groups, called mobs, each led by a large adult male. He warns the others of danger by thumping his big feet.

Just like me
Before you could walk, your parents may have carried you around in a baby carrier. Kangaroo moms do, too—but they have a built-in pouch for that.

Huge **feet** are used for hopping and swimming.

The **tail** is a muscle that works like an extra leg to help with hopping. It is also used for support when the animal is standing.

HUGGABLE?

☐ YES ☒ NO

While they seem soft and playful, kangaroos are expert fighters. They "box" with their arms and kick, too.

The **ears** move and hear sounds from all directions.

The **nose** helps locate food and water.

Small **arms** end in **clawed hands** used to grab grass and plants.

INFO BITES

Name: Eastern Grey Kangaroo

Type of animal: Mammal

Home: Eastern, Southern, Southwestern Australia, plus Tasmania

Size: Does (females) are up to 6 feet tall and 37 to 88 pounds; bucks (males) are up to 7 feet tall and 110 to 146 pounds.

Moving fact: Springing up on powerful hind legs, they can jump 6 feet straight in the air and leap a distance of 25 feet.

Social climbers

Many animals live high up in trees and mountains, or need to climb to reach food or safety. Whether moving from branch to branch or just going up and down, these animals have special talents for getting around.

Serious skills

Baboons have strong arms, hands, and feet. They are expert climbers. They use their fingers and toes to grab the rocky cliffs or trees where they live. They are very strong for their size.

Hold on tight!

Geckos are excellent climbers. Their feet are covered with millions of tiny, sticky hairs called setae. This helps them stick to any surface. They can even climb upside down.

Branching out

Gibbons use their long arms, flexible bodies, and short thumbs to swing from branch to branch. They are fast and agile climbers—the best among mammals that live in trees.

Bungee spider

Jumping spiders catch their food by—you guessed it— jumping on it. They attach a silky string to the place they are standing, then jump. This "safety web" keeps them from falling.

It's a bird! It's a plane!

The southern flying squirrel doesn't actually fly, but it looks like it does. It spreads its arms to form a kind of sail to glide from tree to tree. This squirrel can launch itself from a height of about 60 feet, and glide for more than 160 feet.

Just like me

Some skydivers wear wingsuits known as "flying squirrel suits." These suits help them glide through the air.

INFO BITES

Name: Southern Flying Squirrel

Type of animal: Mammal

Home: North America; forests and woodlands

Size: 8 to 10 inches long, including the tail.

Moving fact: Its sharp claws help it hold on to the bark of a tree before jumping.

Large **eyes** give it good night vision.

The **gliding membrane** is a loose flap of skin between the front leg and back leg.

Fleshy pads on the feet soften the impact on landing.

A flat **tail** helps with steering and changing direction.

SLUMBER-PARTY PAL WORTHY?

[X] YES [X] No

This squirrel is nocturnal and will stay up all night with you. But no one's going to get much sleep!

Making a move

Hop to it!

Lots of animals hop to get from one place to another. Well-developed hind legs give them a fast start on their travels and help them escape danger, too.

South American horned frog

Verreaux's sifaka

Adélie penguins

Earthworm

Diamondback rattlesnake

Garden snail

Blue-winged grasshopper

Red-necked wallaby

Slider jumping spider

Green rat snake

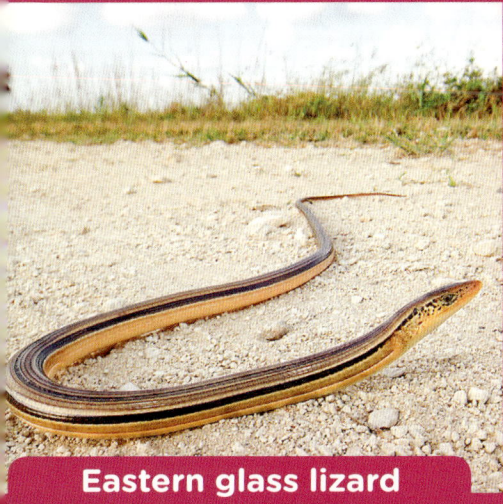

Eastern glass lizard

Banana slug

Slime time!

No legs? No problem! Limbless animals slither on their bellies. Some, like snakes, use scales to pull themselves forward. Others get a smooth ride on their own slime.

Boing! Boing!

Jump! Twist! Do it again! Springboks can leap about 7 feet into the air in a move called "pronking." This helps them evade fast predators like the cheetah.

INFO BITES

Name: Springbok

Type of animal: Mammal

Home: Southwestern Africa

Size: Up to 36 inches tall (at shoulder) and 66 to 100 pounds.

Moving fact: Springboks straighten their legs and arch their backs when they pronk. They pronk to see things around them, to confuse predators, and to attract the attention of other springboks.

Just like me

People get water from fruits and vegetables. When it is hot and dry, springboks eat plants and roots, which hold water, to keep themselves hydrated.

Pocketlike **skin flap** on back opens to show a ridge of white hair while pronking.

Curved **horns** are sharp and useful in battles for territory and mates. Both males and females have horns.

Distinctive **coloring** includes white and dark brown stripes that run from each eye down to the lip.

Hard **hooves** provide protection from rocky ground and prevent sinking down in sandy areas.

TRACK MEET-WORTHY?

☒ YES ☐ NO

Fast runner? Check. Long jumper? Check. This all-around athlete can clear the hurdles and bring home the win.

Catching air

How can frogs jump so high and so far? They use leg muscles and tendons (which connect the muscles to bones) like springs to launch themselves into the air. Frogs can jump high and even in zigzag motions to get from place to place and escape predators.

In the groove

Smooth moves, jerky dances, and other dramatic displays help animals attract mates. These animals have some of the coolest moves in the animal kingdom.

Shake it!

A male peacock spider does a happy dance to attract a mate. He may shake his body, raise his legs, or sway his arms back and forth. It's risky, because if a female isn't interested, she'll try to eat him.

Dance party

When mating season arrives, an entire flock of flamingoes performs a dance. They march together, taking tiny steps and flicking their heads back and forth. When a male and female pair up, they may stay together for years.

Dance competition

Some mating moves are fights between rivals. When two male rattlesnakes are interested in the same female, they do a combat dance. The stronger snake wins, and the loser moves on.

Cuddle up

When roseate spoonbills pair up, they exchange small gifts of sticks. They also dance and clap their bills together.

Animal trackers

Wildlife experts study where and why animals move. This provides information that helps us understand and protect our natural world. Scientists use methods and tools that are safe for the animals to track them.

Band it!

Conservation efforts have helped rebuild the peregrine falcon population in Acadia National Park in Maine. Chicks are fitted with a coded leg band and released. Sightings of the banded birds show where they travel and how long they live.

Tag, you're it

OCEARCH is a nonprofit organization that studies marine animals. To learn where and how fast a great white shark travels, they attach a tag to its dorsal fin. Each time the fin breaks the water's surface, the satellite tag sends a signal showing the shark's location on a map.

Teamwork

Monarch Watch is a joint effort among educators, scientists, and citizens to track the population size and migrations of monarch butterflies. Small stickers placed on the wings contain information people use to report where they found a butterfly.

Radio it in

Some wolves in Yellowstone National Park wear radio collars. This allows experts to study hunting behavior, population, and territory size for different wolf packs in the park.

Home surf

A protected area in Dry Tortugas National Park in Florida is home to loggerhead turtles. Satellite tracking tags let experts know how many turtles live there year-round, and whether the protected area is big enough.

Record breakers

All animals have special skills that help them survive and succeed. Some have record-breaking abilities that set them apart.

LEG IT OUT

When the count is in, millipedes win for the most legs of any animal. They have four legs on each body segment (two on each side), and some have as many as 750 in total. They move their legs in a wavy motion to go forward or backward.

OPEN WIDE

The trap-jaw ant has the fastest bite of all. It can open its clawlike mandibles 180 degrees (half a circle!) and close them on prey (insects) at a whopping 143 miles per hour.

SPRING UP

All cats can jump and pounce. But the puma has super-powerful back legs. It can jump 20 feet up or down a hillside without a running start.

LOW RIDER

When a monitor lizard is on the run, it moves superfast. This type of lizard, called a perentie, can sprint up to 20 miles per hour, making it the fastest lizard recorded.

RAPID RUNNER

A cheetah's excellent eyesight helps it scan the grasslands for prey. Once it spots its dinner, this cat—the fastest of all land animals—can accelerate from 0 to 60 miles per hour in three seconds.

NO-FLY ZONE

Ostriches can't fly through the air, but they can run along the ground at up to 45 miles per hour. They use their powerful feet to push off, and their wings to help change directions.

BALANCE ARTIST

The bharal, also known as the Himalayan blue sheep, is an extreme acrobatic jumper. It leaps from rocky cliff to rocky cliff while keeping perfect balance.

SLITHER SNACK

Snakes have a long, tubelike shape that helps them move. This snake is colorful and tasty!

What you'll need:
- 7 banana slices
- 6 strawberry slices
- 2 whole strawberries for head and tail
- 1 small marshmallow, cut in half
- 2 chocolate coated candies
- Peanut butter or marshmallow cream as "glue"
- 1 small piece of carrot for tongue
- Plastic knife

1. Using the plastic knife, spread peanut butter or marshmallow cream on the fruit slices. Assemble the snake body, alternating banana and strawberry slices.
2. Cut the stem end off the whole strawberries.
3. Place one berry at the front for the head, and one stem end on top of the snake's head. Use the other berry as the tail.
4. Use peanut butter or marshmallow cream to stick on the marshmallow and candy eyes.
5. Add carrot piece for tongue, pressing into berry.

You can make your snake as long or short as you'd like. After all, snakes come in lots of different sizes!

SPEED RACER

Some animals slither and slide. Some leap high and jump far. And others can zip through the water at amazing speeds. If you created an animal superhero, how would it move? Think about ways it would help to be able to jump, fly, dive, hop, wriggle, and run. Then give your superhero animal a name.

MEALTIME FLIGHT

When birds spot something good to eat, they fly in. Make this bird feeder and see who stops by for a meal.

What you'll need:
- 24-inch piece of string
- Pinecone
- Paper plate
- Bird seed
- Spoon
- Peanut butter or vegetable shortening

1. Tie one end of the string around the top of the pine cone.
2. Pour a thin layer of bird seed onto the paper plate.
3. Spoon the peanut butter or shortening on the pinecone. Make sure to cover the entire pinecone. Try not to get it on the string.
4. Roll coated pinecone in the bird seed, pressing it into the seeds to make sure they stick.
5. Hang the pinecone feeder on a tree branch. The long string will help keep squirrels from stealing the seeds.

Watch to see which birds eat the seeds, how they fly to it, and whether they land on it or hover nearby.

Resources

FIND OUT MORE

Learn more about these fascinating animals by reading books, checking out interesting websites, and visiting zoos and museums.

PLACES TO VISIT

Aquarium of the Pacific
Long Beach, CA
aquariumofpacific.org
Learn about the Pacific Ocean and its animal inhabitants at the Aquarium of the Pacific. The aquarium features 19 major habitats and is home to more than 11,000 ocean animals. See how jellyfish float through the water, and watch Magellanic penguins move around in the water and on land.

San Diego Zoo
San Diego, CA
zoo.sandiegozoo.org
In the San Diego Zoo's "Animals in Action," keepers and animals show visitors how exotic animals move around in their habitats. Learn how big cats can navigate a tree while maintaining their balance. And see how zookeepers work with animals' natural abilities to help them move around at the zoo.

Smithsonian's National Zoo
Washington, DC
nationalzoo.si.edu
Admission is free at the National Zoo, where you can see more than 1,500 animals from 300 different species. Visitors can walk along the American Trail and observe animals moving and acting in species-specific ways. Watch gray seals and harbor seals swim, gray wolves climb and play on wood piles, and beavers construct dams. Wade into the Tide Pool with sea stars, barnacles, and mussels.

Jacksonville Zoo
Jacksonville, FL
jacksonvillezoo.org
Watch exotic birds like the yellow-bellied stork and lesser flamingo fly about freely in the River Valley Aviary. See monkeys jump and swing from tree to tree at the lively Plains of East Africa exhibit. This large, open environment is home to cheetahs, elephants, and many other animals.

Lion Country Safari
Loxahatchee, FL
lioncountrysafari.com
Take a drive through seven different areas of Lion Country Safari to discover wild animals, including African lions, wildebeests, impala, ostriches, and more. Safari World offers walk-through exhibits, giraffe feeding, and a petting zoo. Various animals can be seen roaming at the Hwange National Park.

San Antonio Zoo
San Antonio, TX
sazoo-aq.org
At the San Antonio Zoo, you can see ostriches, Grevy's zebra, African crowned cranes, and antelopes gather around the water hole in the African Plains exhibit. In the Amazonia exhibit, spider monkeys hang and swing by their prehensile tails.

Omaha's Henry Doorly Zoo and Aquarium
Omaha, NE
omahazoo.com
Interact with butterflies at the Butterfly and Insect Pavilion, and visit Expedition Madagascar to see a Giant jumping rat. The zoo's largest aquarium includes coral reefs, a polar environment, and a 70-foot shark tunnel where sea turtles and sharks swim all around.

Bronx Zoo
Bronx, NY
bronxzoo.com
The Bronx Zoo offers opportunities to get up close and personal with some of the animals. Take a camel ride in Wild Asia Plaza. And check out the Flight! exhibit to get a close-up look at how birds fly.

CANADA

Calgary Zoo
Calgary, AB
calgaryzoo.com
Watch the eager otters, tigers, and snow leopards during feeding times. And check out the Canadian Wilds to see bears splashing in their ponds and eagles perched high in the treetops. At Penguin Plunge, watch Gentoo, rockhopper, and king penguins dive into chilly water and waddle on the ice.

Toronto Zoo
Toronto, ON
torontozoo.com
More than 5,000 animals live at the Toronto Zoo in exhibits including African Savanna and Tundra Trek. The zoo offers several workshops for students, such as Animal Senses, Animals Classification, and Animal Movement. The Discovery Zone features a Kids' Zoo, and you can learn about endangered species when you ride the Conservation Carousel.

WEBSITES

You can visits all of the zoos and animal centers online to learn more. Here are some additional websites to check out.

discoverykids.com
Check out different animals from around the world, such as sharks and tortoises, in their natural habitats. Play games and watch videos at this entertaining site.

explore.org
Watch animal cams from around the world. You can visit places like the Katmai National Park in Alaska, the Long-eared owls in Montana, Kitten Rescue in California, African River Wildlife in Kenya, or the Ouwehand Park for Polar Bears in the Netherlands.

National Park Service
nps.gov
The National Park Service includes more than 400 different places around the United States. You can see all kinds of wildlife, from wolves in Yellowstone (Wyoming) and manatees in the Everglades (Florida) to spotted owls in Yosemite (California) and beavers in Acadia (Maine). Visit the website to learn all about the different parks and animals that live there, and find cool photos and activities. You can even become a Junior Ranger and learn to explore and protect our natural world.

BOOKS

ANIMAL BITES
Meet amazing animals from around the world in these *Animal Bites* books.

Baby Animals
Explore the lives of all kinds of baby animals, from kittens and puppies to crocodiles and kangaroos. See how they grow, and learn where and how they live. Find out different ways animal experts help baby animals and how to adopt the right pet for you.

Farm Animals
Take a trip to the farm. Learn about farm life, and see how and where farm animals live.

Ocean Animals
Journey through the oceans. Learn about marine animals from around the world, and see how and where they live.

Polar Animals
Travel from the tippy-top of the planet to the very bottom. Learn about the animals that call the North and South Poles home, and see how and where they live.

Wild Animals
Explore the habitats of wild animals around the world. Learn about animals that survive and thrive in the wild, and see how and where they live.

ANIMAL PLANET ANIMAL ATLAS
What is a habitat? What is a food web? Answers to these and hundreds of other questions are answered in a kid-friendly way.

ANIMALS: A VISUAL ENCYCLOPEDIA
Meet more than 2,500 amazing animals in this comprehensive family reference book. It includes more than 1,000 stunning photos!

Glossary

amphibian A cold-blooded animal that starts its life in the water, but lives mostly on land as an adult. Frogs are amphibians.

Antarctic Relating to the South Pole.

arachnid An animal that has main body parts, eight legs, and no antennae. Spiders are arachnids.

Arctic Relating to the North Pole.

burrow A home animals make by tunneling into the ground.

calf The young of some animals. Baby cows, moose, and whales are calves.

coat The hair or fur that covers an animal's body.

colony A group of animals living in one place. Some birds live in colonies.

conservation The protection of animals, plants, and natural resources.

dam A barrier across a river or stream that holds back water. Beavers build dams out of sticks and mud to create a safe home and food supply.

den A small, hollowed area where an animal lives. Bears and badgers live in dens.

dung Solid animal waste, or poop.

▼ **fin** Flat body parts that help fish and aquatic mammals move and balance in the water.

*This orca calf swims by its mother's dorsal **fin**.*

forewings The front two wings of four-winged insects.

habitat The place where an animal usually lives, or an area where different animals live together.

heat pits Holes on a snake's head between the eyes and nostrils. Heat pits help the snake sense the body heat of nearby prey.

herd A group of animals that live, or are kept, together. Reindeer and cows live in herds.

▼ **hover** To hang in one spot in the air, moving only the wings.

*Hummingbirds **hover** above flowers when eating nectar.*

hydrate To add water to something. Animals drink water to hydrate themselves.

inland The inner part of a country or piece of land.

larva The baby, wormlike form of animals that go through metamorphosis. A caterpillar is a butterfly larva.

lodge An animal home built out of sticks and mud. Beavers build lodges in or near the water.

mammal An animal that produces milk to feed its young, has hair on its body, and has a backbone. Humans and polar bears are mammals.

mandible The jaws of an insect.

marsupial An animal that raises its young in a pouch on the mother's belly. Kangaroos, opossums, and wombats are marsupials.

migrate To move from one place to another place, according to the season.

*Millions of wildebeests **migrate** nearly 1,000 miles each year to find fresh food and water.*

mucus A slimy protective substance given off by some animals. Slugs produce mucus to help them slide along the ground without injuring their bodies.

nest A place built to birth and raise young. Many birds, squirrels, and wasps build nests.

nocturnal Active at night. A nocturnal animal sleeps in the daytime.

offspring The children of mother and father animals.

pack A group of animals that lives together. Wolves and dogs live in packs.

pouch A pocket of skin on the belly of female marsupials. The babies live in the mother's pouch after they are born.

pounce To jump on prey.

*Coyotes **pounce** to catch prey underneath the snow.*

predator An animal that hunts and eats other animals.

prey An animal that is eaten by other animals.

range An open land area where animals roam and feed.

reptile A cold-blooded animal that often has scales. Snakes and turtles are reptiles.

rival An animal that competes with another animal for territory, food, or a mate.

saliva A watery substance produced in the mouths of humans and other animals. Saliva helps animals soften and swallow food.

scales Thin, hardened, dry disks that cover the bodies of some animals. Lizards and fish have scales.

school A group of fish.

*Barracudas swim in a **school** to help protect themselves from predators.*

soar To glide through the air using very little wing movement.

spar To fight. In the animal world, sparring is usually between males fighting over mates.

stalk To follow prey silently and without being seen.

talon The sharp claws on the feet of some birds, especially birds of prey.

tusk A long, sharp tooth that sticks out of the mouths of some animals. Elephants have tusks.

wingspan The distance from tip to tip of a bird's fully extended wings.

zigzag To move by changing direction and making sharp turns. Wildebeest move in a zigzag pattern to escape predators.

Index

78

Photo credits

Advisor Michael Rentz, PhD
Lecturer in Mammalogy, Iowa State University

Special thanks to the Time Inc. Books team: Margot Schupf, Anja Schmidt, Beth Sutinis, Deirdre Langeland, Georgia Morrissey, Megan Pearlman, Melodie George, and Sue Chodakiewicz.

Special thanks to the Discovery and Animal Planet creative and licensing team: Denny Chen, Tracy Conner, Elizabeta Ealy, Robert Marick, Doris Miller, Sue Perez-Jackson, and Janet Tsuei.

Produced by
Scout Books & Media Inc
President and Project Director
Susan Knopf
Writer Dorothea DePrisco
Editor Ellen Stamper
Project Manager
Brittany Gialanella
Copyeditor Beth Adelman
Proofreader Michael Centore
Indexer Andrea Baron
Designer Dirk Kaufman
Prepress by Andrij Borys Associates, LLC

LIBERTY STREET

Published by Liberty Street, an imprint of Time Inc. Books
225 Liberty Street
New York, New York 10281

LIBERTY STREET is a trademark of Time Inc.

ISBN 10: 1-61893-179-2
ISBN 13: 978-1-61893-179-5

First edition, 2017

Printed and bound in China

1 TLF 17

Time Inc. Books products may be purchased for business or promotional use. For information on bulk purchases, please contact Christi Crowley in the Special Sales Department at (845) 895-9858.

To order Time Inc. Books Collector's Editions, please call (800) 327-6388, Monday through Friday, 7 a.m.-9 p.m., Central Time.

We welcome your comments and suggestions about Time Inc. Books. Please write to us at:
Time Inc. Books

Attention: Book Editors

P.O. Box 62310
Tampa, Florida 33662-2310